MW01656990

IN EVERYTHING, BIRDS

poems

by

Debbi Brody

ISBN: 978-1-936923-13-7

First Edition 2015

Cover Art & Design by Devey Napier

Village Books Press Cheyenne, Oklahoma

Acknowledgments

I have so many people to thank, from workshop leaders and attendees to living poets and many who came before, informing my poetic lineage and greatly impacting my writing style, philosophy and literary yearnings.

I wish to thank Joan Logghe, Judyth Hill and Anita Skeen for their constant support in my endeavors. Many thanks to Teresa Gallion, who convinced me to come out of the closet with my writing, to go public. It has changed my life.

I thank my writing groups for keeping my pen rolling even when I think it's the last thing I wish to do, especially Rachelle Woods, Mary McGinnis, Terra Pressler, Moriah Williams and Gary Moody.

As my sister, Wendy Kapp, suggested I must thank her as well. Although she does not appear directly in this collection, for many early years she was my muse, and I believe the self-examination she was responsible for in me, made me a better, more complete person and writer. I give thanks to my mother for the gene of creativity and the validation that a creative life is a legitimate way to go.

A very special thanks to my publishers at Village Books Press who took a chance on me in 2006 and published my first "real" book, *Portraits in Poetry*. Their press has grown and developed into an award-winning book factory. I am humbled that all these years later, they still believe in me enough to do it again!

Last but far from least, many thanks to my son, Dylan Brody, for all the positive reinforcement and emotional support. To my husband and best friend, Bob Brody, for knowing when I need to sprawl out with books and papers all over the house, sometimes even with papers taped to the dining room walls, and for never complaining about that or the hours of "alone" and quiet time I need when reading, writing and revising.

I love you all.

The following poems have been published in slightly different versions in the journals listed:

"A Possible Abandonment," *Miriam's Well Poetry, Land and Beyond,* 2010

"In Everything, Birds," *Ibid.*

"Cycles," *Not Drowning Waving*, Piñon Press, January 2009

"Eight Ways In," *Contemporary American Voices Poetry Journal*, September 2009

"Harmony," *Not Drowning Waving*, Piñon Press, 2008

"Thailand; A Double Sonnet," *Not Drowning Waving*, Piñon Press, May 2008

"A Woman Listens to the Paul Winter Consort," *Santa Fe Literary Review*, 2008

"Hummingbird Turquoise," published as "Green," *Central Avenue*, February 2007

"Ode to a Mexican Oracle," *Santa Fe Literary Review*, 2007

"Hidden Fiction," *Central Avenue*, April 2006

"Big Dream Pantoum," *Central Avenue*, December 2005 and Miriam's Well Poetry

Table of Contents

I am no bird; and no net ensnares me: I am a free human being with an independent will.

Charlotte Brontë, *Jane Eyre*

Thailand: A Double Sonnet

The King of Thailand/Siam is no Yul Brynner.
When he says, *Gorillas love jungle,*

he's not talking about primates.
When he says, *Bears are seldom seen*

in the forest, he's not talking about
Chicago or football. The king,

a benevolent, well-loved grandfather
in a land without speed limits

and with instant incarceration
for slander of his royal highness.

When Gandhi said, *You can tell every-*
thing you need to know about a culture

by how they treat their dogs, he means,
watch how they treat their dogs.

***

Wrens peck at pumpkin and papaya
offerings to Ganesh, just as he wishes.

Sticky rice encased in palm leaf, held
together by a staple. East meets West.

Left hand sprouts snow peas,
right hand grows roses.

When Johnny says *tension*, he means
a spider on the water's surface,

when he says *lunch,* he means fresh
bamboo and morning-glory leaves.

When Bob says, *Let's go to Umpang,* he means
a 160-kilometer game of chicken, no brakes,

the good side of the road no worse
than the bad side. Not a math problem.

Anxiety Dreams

Her student arrives for tutoring
halfway through the semester, unsure
of the course title, the professor's name
or the details of the assignment except
that it has something to do with nature.

The student lives my high-anxiety dreams;
time for finals and I have forgotten to attend
class, opening night and I have missed the rehearsals,
customers complain and I forget to go to their
table, take their order, deliver their food.

Carol said, *List the objects in recurring dreams,*
see what they have to tell you, what they want you to know,
become their voice, write for them.

Dinnerware, curtains, textbooks, test papers,
mailboxes, faded receipts, round white wooden
tables, playbooks, footlights, heat lamps, sunny-
side-up eggs, hallways with numbered doors.
Red-vinyl notebook, intense color, dull finish,
held by tan hands. Cold eggs, salted and peppered,
maybe spat on by the cook, his enormous bare biceps
rippled in stretch marks, reverse tattoos on deep
brown skin. Hallways with miles of doors,
top half framing mottled translucent glass,
gold-stenciled numbers, smell dentist's office,
doctor's office.

Where are my lollipops, Sleeping Beauty and Goofy
plastic figures, broken-stick caramel apples with peanuts?

Textbook, playbook, will I know what's inside without
reading? Do I know the rules, the sequence of events,
when I should walk on and off stage, speak or remain silent? Can
I read the prompters' lips, see the cue cards, see over
the shoulder of the test-taker in front of me who may or may not
know the name of our professor.

A Possible Abandonment

We pray for the return of the House finch's frightened flight,
check through the six-by-four inch window in the front door,
expect her sudden ascent at our passages in and out of the house.

The chicks squeak volubly, now they are as big as a hen's egg,
their mother we have missed for over a day. We check at
midnight,
2 a.m., 8 a.m. Dylan thinks he saw her sitting, but didn't
have his glasses on. By the time we find ours, she is gone,
if she was ever there at all. The hatchling on the right sticks his
ropey
head out over the edge of the chili ristra, the other two reach
necks straight into the air, beaks wide, tongues rapid.

We cannot let three birds starve in our entryway, we have zero
tolerance for parental neglect. Yet the vet has not returned
our calls for sugar-water eye-dropper recipes. We keep one
eye out the window and wait for the phone to ring.

Argentina 2010

1. Buenos Aires

Primal Bee Sweeping at the Museum of Contemporary
Latin American Art,

Jimi and Janis play at the Krishna Restaurant,

Warhol everywhere, caught in the iconography
of his time until he became an idol. Brilliant
movement of the soul includes Marilyn's mole.

Dining, a late-middle-aged couple deep-tongues
in the back of a restaurant.   Under a two-top,
a young man slides low in his chair, separates
his date's legs with his knees. Paris of South America.

A lavender storm night. Angel of Silence divides
the moon in two, one part for Borges to share
with Che, the other half for Lorca and Neruda.
On subways, Saramago and Allende. People
still read books in this land of unsalted butter and free
plastic surgery.

Angel of Fire speeds through chests in a porteño
Thai restaurant.

2. The River

Palms, willows, reeds, geese on the Tigres.
Stilt houses called *never say never,*
grocery boats, bus boats, sunken ships.

3. Transformation

Some carbon life returns as oil,
some magma hits the surface as peridot,
some hotels recompose as flea markets,
some rocks come back as thrown stone.

Ars Poetica

To be a William Carlos Williams
and write tercets, three lines, each piece
anapest accent all the way through

or like Lorca to lyrically
list out many parts of live bodies
next, the lost animals and flowers,

finally sing wind through my lost
places. Girl, shoulder, forehead, boy, not
least a pigeon-*paloma*, iris

turtle, a lily takes us to hallways,
bed, banks, a thousand windows to
our waiting grave, *broken, wasted waltz.*

Assault and Recurring Dreams; An Introduction

I

At age nine, I chased
a rubber ball down four steps
leading to a cellar staircase
under the apartment across the alley.

He was no older than fourteen,
tried to shove my face down by forcibly
pushing my body to the concrete,
holding my hair as he shoved
me to his zipper, trying to undo
his pants with his other hand.

Victorious this one time,
I hauled ass out of there,
ran up the gray back stairs
and through the kitchen door.

II

For forty-four years I have dreamed
of being forced by unknowable
circumstances into dark and confusing
alleys where I must rescue myself from dim
and deadly danger, taking wrong
turns in parking garages, crossing
over yellow paths on perfect lawns
to take shortcuts in an effort to find
a less dangerous alley. I try
to get to a train through a risky
neighborhood. If I succeed, I ride the El
to a station at the corner of Chicago
and Main over a newsstand.

I walk triangular streets, lost
in another bad part of town.

By age fourteen, with multiple,
unshared burdens of assaults
and abuses, I dream I stand
on a trapezoidal grass plot
in front of a dingy, pillared
church across from my home.

III

I still pray the teenage boy, who
failed to get me where he wanted,
gave up violence and never hurt
another little girl. Not true of my next
attacker, he served three long terms,
spending more than 30 years
in several prisons for molesting
other little girls after he
was done with silent me.

IV

Alleys in all configurations;
under gray skies, with and without
yellowish-white garage doors open
or shut between brick structural stanchions,
the sun beating down so bright *I can see*
humidity in the air. I drop groceries, run
through yards, struggle through fences
between houses only to find myself
back in the same alley, surrounded
by tall apartments, a scratched white-
and-pink rubber ball left behind
on the asphalt while I ascend between
the surrounding structures—
and fly.

Spell of Undoing Epigenetics

I rid myself of pogroms,
diasporas, Holocaust, vigilance.
I rid myself of The Inquisition,
of spitting pork in hand
to surreptitiously drop it
to the Lord's dogs under the table.

I rid myself of anxiety,
fear of insanity, the worry
gene. I rid myself of generations
of dead babies, hiding in forests,
under floorboards, in root cellars,
unable to save my children.

I rid myself of addiction to tobacco,
to Facebook, to sour cream, to books,
to overanalyzing, to overplanning.

I gift myself a new, unfettered DNA,
slice the heads off the apocalyptic
horsemen before they enter my realm,
attack the thieves before they enter the cave.

I encode myself with whalebone,
migratory flight, antelope grace,
cheetah speed, duck fidelity,
and the circulating water of the world.

At Last, A Poem My Husband Likes!

I am a cannibal for your love,
a willing victim on starry night
after moon filled night.

You, my forever
hot taco, have got me
steamed up with never-ending
desire. Satiation has a new
kind of flip-flopping definition.

The orchid of my heart
is carpeted in variegated
petals that form you,
the knitted scarf that warms
my vulnerable neck.

I become a subversive
coyote howling in lust.
Scratch the itch, watch
it become deeper, more
wanton.

Leave me be, go to Turkey.
Dance with burka-clad women
who cannot be touched. Go
to all the countries where women
are invisible. Remember, come
home, see me, touch me.

A Too Long Prose Poem

Can't stop looking out, listening for sirens, for owls passing through clouds like steamed milk. We're not seventeen, yet she still chases dead turtles. Been idiopathic so long it looks like normal, like lemonade. Every generation's incomprehensible technology, elders say, destroys culture; moving wheels, frightening things, radios corrupt, telephone the devil's work, i-Pods and texts, connections that disconnect. We, no different than our antecedents, perhaps taller, longer-lived in the same misapprehensions. Who moves forward, beyond us? Her plan, her pain, her sickness, never knew it was a game, a contest, stood no chance to win, as if we are particles, flower petals, solar dust, unkempt hair, unlined paper. It's all a plaza dance, we pick the spirits and the order they will dance into the ceremonies. I want Warrior Woman, Spider Woman, Squash Guardian, Sun Kachina, Mixed-Up Dancer. Koshare spitting watermelon seeds intercedes at every turn around the plaza, Sacred Clowns as good as any hanged man, any fool, any harlequin, better than a dead rabbit, better than any rabbit I never killed.

Autumn's Octaves

Five golden leaves in a tree of green, old
gray bark, crevices deep as a thumb,
red, beige, brown, umber, sepia leaves
in gardened grass. Last year's leaves,
mulch against sandstone rocks,
a cushion for new growth, food
for *chamisa* and *cholla.* Vinca curls
inward in autumn's night chill, ferny

willow grows dark, naked, still except
for the scratch of a Canyon towhee,
the rapid ruffling of its mate. Late
summer asters fold into a broom,
wild alfalfa goes to seed. Bindweed
spreads long arms, drops pods
for next spring. One orange globe-
mallow blooms low to the ground.

Deer tracks in the mud.

A Woman Listens to the Paul Winter Consort

Head tilts back, gray streaks, straight, black
even bangs and razored, shoulder-length hair.
Glasses, horizontal, lacquered rectangles
low on a dappled, flat nose. She unfolds
fragile foil on imported chocolate,
snaps off a sliver, small as the white
crescent on her thumb, folds back the silver
as precise as origami, sucks dark,
bitter candy, like a calamity, like a swan.

Barn Swallows

Birds migrate through my backyard, Yellow warbler, tanager,
Canyon towhee. Days get longer, mornings arrive earlier.

Yesterday, a blue egg, black speckles in the gravel,
today, gray-flecked shell on the concrete.

This year, I planted six days late, learning
to slow down, to not play superwoman.

We are all birds, Barn swallows making our homes
in the space left by missing bricks and broken gutters.

It's the War

She writes God as a madman and man as the devil.

Until it happens to you, it doesn't seem like a big deal.

He knows when others think of him, they will think of the accident and the dead boy, too.

When swimming through filthy mucus, time clogs every pore, obscures breath and vision.

We feel safer knowing where the last bullet, one of eight, hit, marked by a pink ribbon.

Little plastic bubbles didn't make her happy, so she put an end to it.

Difficult, perfect feet.

Siblings keep us young through permanent, preadult relationship functions.

There is a story with the coral necklace skittering to be told.

Planets line up on her bracelet like pearls, yellow diamonds, and one small ruby.

Beauty, her secret weapon until he says, *Darling, would you like to be redundant tonight?*

As exposed as a fat woman running naked on the set of the Jerry Springer Show.

Light a lavender candle on a glass plate beaded with a Jewish star.

Don't evaluate your behavior based on its resemblance to sanity.

Keep things from boiling over; three birds in a cage, one in another.

One day, the second candle will be lit.

TOMORROW, EVERYTHING WILL BE TRUE.

I won't be your word-runner.

We bargain our way through small spaces in the kitchen.

Their house, a mirage, a flash, a monument, a brief marriage.

Explain the difference between a baby and a chicken.

Reborn as an autumn leaf.

I expect bail-bonders to wear pinky rings.

You've been eating my brain again.

Possessed, she is inside and sometimes flickers out convincingly from behind her own eyes.

Bean sprout, your ability to help others may not be seen by all.

I did a suicide dance for thirty-one years, killed myself every day so I could be alive for now, a seven seed pomegranate heart robed in a garnet bursary.

Bent from the Neck

A room formed by the trick of three white walls, each humming and banging with hollow doors. The child's feet dangle into a hall. Above floats a crated blue goddess, waiting to burst out, Kali-black, skulls' head necklace and yellow eyes. The unwind of perilous laughter, a dance of attention replete with the blurry echo of crows. Perhaps an oily twitch of night and too much food. Somewhere an amalgam of scattered light and frosted trees. A baby flings meaty arms around her close-eyed mother, clings tight to her sweaty neck. Somewhere a peasant, somewhere hunger, somewhere a cheetah runs across a veldt. Elsewhere the sun muscles over a blue-checkered picnic table floating in a flood-filled arroyo.

Big Dream Pantoum

Walking into a big dream, hands gentled around
a Gouldian finch, lavender chin,
every line of color separation pure, no transition.
Drop him in a white, wrought-iron cage on a table.

A Gouldian finch, lavender chin
becomes a purple bucket on the floor.
Drop him in a white, wrought-iron cage on a table.
The bird, now a mouse, hangs by his sharp jaw,

becomes a purple bucket on the floor,
clings to my index finger. Rasp him into writhing.
The bird, now a mouse, hangs by his sharp jaw,
scraped into a bucket by a whitewashed, wooden board.

Clinging to my index finger, rasped into writhing,
a rat climbs the panel, hangs from my wrist with serrated teeth,
scraped into a bucket by a whitewashed wooden board.
Black-and-white striped snakes braid through my hair.

A rat climbs the panel, hangs from my wrist with serrated teeth.
No one helps. Sound familiar? The beast grows.
Black-and-white striped snakes braid through my hair.
I tell the dream story standing in the kitchen, packing lunch.

No one helps. Sound familiar? The beast grows.
Drinking coffee, he says, *Seems like you're feeling things—*
I tell the dream story standing in the kitchen packing lunch.
Are out of control. I laugh and say, *No kidding, Batman.*

Drinking coffee, he says, *Seems like you're feeling things—*
walking into a big dream, hands gentled around,
are out of control. I laugh and say, *No kidding, Batman,*
every line of color separation pure, no transition.

Breaking from the Inside

Random-access memory
to a hiccup of a head slammed against a car-door frame
to menstruating in a moldy sleeping bag
to pulling porcupine needles from a wild dog's snout
to hair on fire in a basement candle-making factory
to an elevator to the attic -- Pink Ripple, cameras, lights, action
to the trunk of a Chevy in the middle of a hay field
to plucking a newly slaughtered chicken
to single roses held over naked young women
to silver rings that spell *agape* in English and Greek
to strawberry-flavored rolling papers and carrot-cheese soup
to pantyhose and headbands
to lawns getting mowed and knives being drawn
to locking doors with latches
to cupboard drawers full of cockroaches
to motorcycle rides without helmets or shoes
to hitchhiking down mountains and through towns
to slicing potatoes for fresh French fries and filling
        hot dog buns with relish tomato onion ketchup
        leave out the dog
to abandoned clapboard houses on the good side of the city
to beanbag chairs
to garages converted to dens of iniquity
to thinking it's love when it's convenient
to thinking it's inconvenient when it's love
to not being afraid
of flesh-colored monsters
of men with beards and moustaches
of white men with big Afros
of men with gold teeth
of being thrown to the wolves.

Can You Haiku?

ice bucket
dry on the dresser
dead moth inside

caterpillar cocoons
above the hall light
each year its twin appears

in the alfalfa
horse dung
a snake slips by

on the gravel path
to your door
a smiley face eraser

darkroom chemicals
smell less pungent now
air filters whisper

young Republican
worries about his children
votes for Obama

round pyramids
Mexico a spirit place
others drink tequila

raven wings flap
the sound of a ceiling fan
a tail hangs from its beak

the sky is cloudy
barometric pressure drops
airplane overhead

on the sofa
head tipped back
the dog snores

ground trembles beneath
lamps sway above the table
they're at it again

A Cataclysm of Hens

The hens are gone, I spotted a chicken foot
stuck in the fencing at the house before yours
and knew right away. Half the coop smashed,
feathers everywhere, and your retriever sports
a bandaged leg, his head in a cone
he tries to shake off. I know it's not the dogs
fault. I pull my small black terrier's nose
out of the yellow dirt where she searches
for cat poop to eat.

On the drive home, NPR reports on new-
fangled efforts to save the ecologically specific
Gila trout from the ash and future mud slides
of New Mexico's largest wildfire. They shock
the river to stun, capture and remove the fish
to a safer environment. The man from Fish & Wildlife
has dedicated half his life to these little cannibals.

He earns less per year than the deductions
the Romney's take for their quarter horse,
who competed and won a ribbon this week
in a national dressage event, whatever
that might be. I'll write in the name
of the Fish & Wildlife guy on my 2012 ballot
or maybe the name of one of the dead hens.

Cats Can Fly

Revive our faith in caresses and counterweights, evoke
a desire in us to climb until the limb snaps, to leap
like a stubborn sailor from a church steeple
just as it collapses in fire or waits, silent
as a prodigal bird offering a found poem,
a single seed, a sprig of blossoming apricot.

My pelvis leaps at nature's invocation,
yearns to turn my lost taproot
into an archipelago of mother wit
and carving tools, to shake me off track,
stumbling into a guileless, supernova midnight.

Cycles

Reaping skeleton abandons fruits
of summer to waste in winter's snow.
Death decamps six times in six months,
pruning, diverting the past into a gully
of future, magnificent with runaway
fertility and forgetful fields.

Sun falls on lotus as she spreads pale
petals to welcome Rock dove, pigeon,
mariposa and *chuparosa*.
An injured robin recovers in a cage
with ten powder-blue parakeets,
it's mate clings madly to the outside.

Spring ascends in triumph, a chariot's
prance into light. Swords cut the reins,
horses scatter, hurtle, bounce, gallop
like stars in an abundant, indigo night.

Cargo

Tough leather sent on a platter
rolls into industrial flame.
Paper burns off in flaps, edges
crisp, faceless, illuminated,
toothless, gnashing.

Out of heat a waitress grabs
four plates, balances them
along her left arm. A steep
exaggeration calls her, *rescue,*
help, succor, calls this ephemera
we wade and sift through,
basket of joy, parcel of destiny.

We wait, we hunt, we pray
for the tide to come in, for the other
shoe not to drop, for a plume
of smoke to transform the funeral
pyre into a next life, into an iridescent,
incandescent peacock.

Color

Because some things don't deserve forgiveness,
I don't expect desert birds to wear bright blue,
but they do – Indigo buntings, jays, bluebirds.

When I decided there was no such thing
as gray, I saw blue in the rain, red
in silvered plywood, yellow in your hair.

Containment at Forty Percent

In a no-apricot, no-lilac year
imagine is the word sitting alone.

Pyrocumulus rains useless virga,
a system of dry-on-dry. Trees, prey
for fire, hold no expectations, unfurl
into white-and-black charcoal or into
winded leaf. All ways lead to carbon.

We breath carbon monoxide and ash,
flee like deer from fire, nitrogen
starved enchantment. A bleeding, bonded
bridge to nowhere, a.k.a. everywhere
and the canyon between, beyond rage,
red before the beloved night, laces wings
across the sky, plentiful and cool
as the scent of laughing, besotted ravens,
wild coyote disputing territory. Run
cantankerous bedrock, lava yourself
into symmetry and sea salt.

Curse Laid on by a Jealous Woman

We start at 8:00 p.m., no matter who is here—
Zoe, La Loca, the stocking in a still life,
Little Timmy, my son's bones, her
father's ashes, poison-pitted plums.

The amoeba represents a tear in
Space—who needs linear anyway?
Where?   Time?   More?   I want to take
you apart, affectation by affectation.

I want to loose you into a million
particles of particulate, unseeable
by anyone. Your pristine white
teeth, your perfect insults, your

hands evaporate off men who do
not belong to you, barely belong
to themselves. Hike an overripe
forest with your too-tall husband.

Take your precious rhyming poems,
like a pigeon, rat of the sky, crap on
unsuspecting passersby with your
ulcerated, infected, puncture-wound tongue.

Dream Time

I attain enlightenment in sleep,
including an understanding
of the time-space continuum
as a simultaneity.

I find my totem animals in sleep,
an Arctic wolf, African cheetah,
Great Horned owl, before the
shouting begins.

Carried away, crying while asleep
in the arms of a handsome ocelot,
I rock an old, ninety-pound, black
woman on my lap, feel her ironed
and oiled hair against my chin.
I tease and cuddle her, though
the other animals feel she is too
famous for this kind of casualness.

Predictability and the battle
against it look identical in sleep,
the best stories start or end with birth
or death.   Still, I won't enter a dark
room containing mirrors.

Think of when you made time,
while you slept, stand still.
Some of your brilliance went un-lost,
Milk-white in a river of yellow sand.
Puzzle the image.   Who are you?

Eight Ways In

I Dante

Walk deep inside your pain, swim in it, wash in it,
gargle it. Step out of it, let wind dry your body,
leave the salt to irritate, rub off your dead skin.
At night your perspiration allows the right
amount to dissolve and soak back in.

II Saints

The crazy man and the saint see eagle swim with fish,
fish fly with eagle. The insane and the enlightened
watch auroras expand and contract around distant planets.
The mad and the martyr are pulled by gravity,
hear God's voice from barbwire and bushes,
meet God on mountaintops and when they sleep.

III Matzo

A poem is like matzo, we want to share the shape of world,
of asolitude. We knead water and flour, it rests, catches
yeast from the air. Let it lie, create gaseous space.
There is never time enough before we must stamp
it down, hard fists, bring it raw to the harsh sun.
It dries brittle and flat.

IV Pilgrim

The pilgrim tastes dirt, rips her garment, starves her body,
chants her prayers. When she stumbles, she is embraced
by arms she does not feel, held by the one she does not know,
the one she seeks.

V Spin

We spin the gold-and-silver infinitesimal thread, pulled up
from earth, an unending root, wrap it around ourselves,
a Möbius-built breathing cocoon. A pod, a buffer
as we twirl our way out of and into the infinite.

VI Truth

What did I tell you about eagles, fish, wind, abandon, water,
salt, bread, God? None of it is true. Only the split moment
my breath combines with yours—enlightenment.

VII Anger

Paint chipped from the adobe wall, like your anger,
shows the troweled, well-nursed mud beneath.
Dissolution, unspun irritant emanates from
an exposed space, fills the room. A concussion,
a contusion shaped like two hands praying.

VIII Rumi

I want to write like Rumi. No, I want to be Rumi,
drink from his cup, twirl on his feet, hear the reeds
speak. Commune with ghosts and owls. Stumble
home in the rain, soaked in God.

Envy

The mockingbird poses
as a thrasher, sings
for the Mourning dove
who sings to its mate.

Pull spines from the cone,
reveal the hard shelled nut
still to crack.

Did the paper whites bloom?

Love does not include provisions.

Fall in a High-Desert Home

Hens lay less, too much
zucchini becomes excess
butternut. The air aromatic
with roasting green chili,
and fiery red strung in *ristras*.
A new garlic braid hangs
in the kitchen window.

Mr. Romero, in plaid flannel
comes down from Pecos
in a classic blue Chevy clunker,
wheelbarrows piñon, oak,
and pine into piles out back,
splits last year's large logs
to fit in the burner.

We battle with humidifier filters.
We wrap the boiler in its blanket,
tape plastic sheeting over windows,
drain and cover the swamp cooler.
No leaves to rake.

The Dance Within

The dance inside,
raw and purposed
by wet leaves,
the moon turns slowly
like a hip.

Which birds double
as religious icons,
the list almost endless,
like our sense of temperature,
of heat.

For three seconds a man's
spirit whooshes by,
only a good father
when saying, Good-bye.

What do people say
in the beast, in the belly
of abstraction
where knuckles knock
wood on a podium
of speedy speech.

In the airport, pain
floats, grieving parents,
disintegrated partners,
battered children,
crippling self-doubt,
undirected anger.

We call this Happy Holidays.

Fire

Because he is the king of These Sorts of Things,
he manages small economies of coal and gas,
of stubbornness and reason. Some humans
and some dogs wear bells around their collars
to alert others to their presence.

What can she do to keep the omnivorous
raccoons out of the chicken coop? No bird
should nest in something so unstable.
Tornadoes start with a drop in isobars,
also known as pressure. *And your little dog, too.*

She is just a child, but she nearly ran
over a man on his bicycle as she sped
through the busy parking lot. I watch
the blood-red sun set through smoke.
When she reached in and pulled her diapered
infant from the backseat, I nearly had a word
with her.   Instead, I lit a cigarette.

Radioactive waste in the Valles Caldera
and lead tailings in the Pecos River. Waste, waste
everywhere in New Mexico, only fire will cleanse it.

First Day of Spring

Apricot blossoms, snow
equinox afternoon chaos.

Scrub jay pulls rose hips, Canyon
towhee flees Mourning dove.

From Chinese elm, wind
rips a House finch nest.

Persistent, ancient orders
rebuild. Last year's fruit
germinates beneath frosted soil.

For Ann W.

She wants broadening, urgent poems.
Are you a thrasher or a sparrow?
Be both, a benediction.
Here are words for spell-casting,
words that begin and end in vowels
opening any way they can:
idea
ignite
atmosphere
imagine
aroma
apple
intense
intimate
imitate

Thank you for saving
space for imagination.
Cry for beauty, cry for dust.

For John Phillip Santos

Because time is circular, worlds
before, fiery and star-like,
worlds beyond, stony and cold,
stand as much ours as the place
we call *this world.*

Because omnipresent gates to everywhere,
every when include our bodies, we live
on all sides of the fence. Eyes inform
backs, arms embrace feet.

Because we have mixed blood,
wars rage inside, no matter
the gate we enter—
the Cossack and the Jew,
the Indio and the Spaniard,
the Neanderthal and the Homo sapiens,
the duchess and the handmaid,
the Buddha and the supplicant.

Like blind doulas, we live by feel.
The baby has albino hairs
scattered through thick black
and we attend perpetual creations.

Smiles suggest trees, especially
saplings and paisley-charcoal swirls
of forest, birds and pungent loam
beneath fallen leaves and blinking,
scattered light.

The Field in Your Heart

The field in your heart
holds a strong wind and the thunder
of our elliptical course through the galaxy.

The field in your heart
holds marigolds, chrysanthemums,
daisies and pansies hidden
in a low lying fog.

The Field in Your Heart says
Rest here, this is not the wrong house,
you are not lost in the cottonwoods.
Blind yourself to darkness and deception,
rest your eyes on the swallow winging
across your aorta.

Gone

More dove than rattler,
more owl, less coyote
when you're away
I don't floss enough,
watch too much TV,
sleep more than I should.

The big dog drags sheets,
pillows, blankets off the bed
into the hall. You have

been gone twelve days, nine
to go. The kids text, email
about Thanksgiving. Cooking

for one, I look in the fridge
and wonder if the post-
modern adage, *A vege-*
table is better than a man,
holds any truth.

Gum-Tree Seed

A puffer fish of a tree's seedpod, end of an ogre's cudgel,
a syncopated cacophony of baby birds singing, heads
back, mouths open wide. Escher's dream of a seed
folding in on itself, a Mõbius of pattern and balance.

Likely to draw blood if contact is tight,
openness through small spaces, protective
barrier to keep out what might crush or invade
internal space, a lack of judgment of inner self.

Happy Holidays

Mahogany, a physics equation,
an unsubstantial, aphasic, chemical vibration.
Waves in a fishbowl, a burden of pi.
Is that what you mean by delirium tremens,
by the difference between senility and Alzheimer's,
fear of both the same.

Fear of hocus pocus.
Today a snow shoe,
a *chimenea* full of birdseed,
a wreath of succulents
for a theorem or proof.
150 percent bulletproof
for holidays, for turkeys dressed
in foil bikinis, mother in diapers,
perfumed boys, poison coma toys.
Is that what you mean by ugly winners?

Harmony

" You are the music, while the music lasts."
--T.S. Eliot

I.

He sits in symphony hall, itchy wool suit,
audience to rehearsal.

She rides a squat man's shoulders,
sees Joplin wail at Ravinia Park.

He wakens to early morning
chord repetitions, no tempo, all structure.

She plays all the parts in Prokofiev's
Peter and the Wolf.

He joins a long table of twenty,
featuring a one hundred-dollar bottle of wine,
a minuet on the reel-to-reel.

She sits on a quilt, a half-clothed
family picnic on the living room floor,
Rubber Soul on the turntable.

II.

In harmony we birth ourselves.
Like the echo of timbals,
we vibrate, oscillate, a web of rhythm.
Music—timeless energy, divine
power. A gong reverberates,
its own duet in counterpoint,
aubade to evensong.

Hidden Fiction

What kind of writing hides in midwestern
Mud-blue clouds, high in a desert sky?

What kind of writing hides in free-
wheeling ravens, rats in their beaks?

What kind of writing hides in alfalfa,
ducks into scrub brush at mesa's edge?

One stark minute a starling lyric,
a poem played on a new pool table,

hot asphalt humming like a wavering
oasis, an ode spinning out of orbit.

Hummingbird Turquoise

An illusion of refracted light
registered on rods by absence
in the spectrum. Our last
good time, a turquoise hummingbird
and Sandhill cranes, Snow
geese shouting into sunrise.

Sin and no shame.

Wrens and finches fly from
grapevine to trumpet.
Their flight more honest
than our migratory conversation.
I may not tell and you may not
listen. Once, you were whole.

This time, try to love yourself

as deeply as you love sick men.
All my uncried tears, just
swallowed fear. Colorblind
absorb the same transmissions
on a different kind of cone receptor.
Do all fully sighted see turquoise

or any color the same as each another?

I Don't Have Much to Say Today Except

We improvise our lives,
conjure vestiges of incense
in the agony of azure skies,
try to erase or swallow
the pebble engraved
with injury, or augment
the stone carved
with magpie and eagle.

We pray to idols, intone
eternal abundance, arrive
at the opera vowing
adoration to earth,
to every apple.

In Everything, Birds

Last month, chased by a yellow finch,
raven flew, mole in mouth.

Last week, a wren's severed wing
beneath the back stairs.

Yesterday, a dead Calliope
hummingbird on the path.

Last night, a swallow lunged
at the windshield.

Today, a fledgling grackle
limps in the grass.

Tonight, ride the back of Al-Buraq,
do not tie her to a wall, temple, or hitching post.
Her peacock-feathered beast's body soars
for the multitudes of women, lost goddesses.

What comes down
may also fly up, flame
red on a blackbird's wing.

Instructions

Go to the sacred room
in the former Elks Lodge.
Join hands, tongues out.
Pull together, arms up.
Pull apart, arms stretch.

Go to the museum, the room
where Mr. New burned his last
sage, feathered by an owl's wing.

Sit in light, sing until you scrape
the top of your throat open to sky.
Wait for rapid water, listen.

Life, a Plate, a Knife

Broken ego on a plate,
slice the lobes left and right,
grey jelly, amorphous mass
of nasty, leave reptilian stems
to tangle. Trade for rare
and common glass. Colors
hover blue at base of skull,
feet sift amber light to dirt,
an iridescent possibility,
a song unsold, a thousand
million paper cranes, a zillion
googol of eternity balance
random on edge of knife.
That's life.

Longing for the Full May Moon

Wander out on cactus-flecked mesa
like all broken hearts before,
stare up at heaven, beg
the moon goddess Selene to send
a charm to calm and cool a rare
and brutish spirit.

Crescent mother abandons us again,
will not visit this dry and tender whore.
She organizes spring meadows,
drops hawks, stars, radishes and lizards
throughout her cosmos in quiet, secret
ceremony. She breathes pearls into oceans,
corn into earth and bridges into cities.
She floods empty vessels with wine
and presses dreams inside wolves.

Stay near the door, await
her honeyed garments.

Letter to the Earth

I know nothing else but miracles.
—Walt Whitman

Generosity of orange yellow leaves
Green-veined on cottonwood trees,
Steller's jay on conifer branches,
grey burro grazes at the base
of an alfalfa field, three-legged
heeler nips after flatbed.
Sun disappears behind multilayered
mesa, contrast of sky and rock.
Easels set in parking lots and *llanos*
paint miracles, pens rub paper
in classrooms, record miracles.

Looking for Hope

Ponderosa, apricot, dead, dying.
Where do birds find water?
You transcendentalize into lightning
with nowhere to go but down
into the beetle die-off until there's nothing
left to burn. Wait one hundred years
for aspen forest, lover of potash,
ants, potassium and nitrogen.

Time, an imaginary construct, the sense
of standing firm, still, when truth flies
at incomprehensible speeds. The apex,
a whisper, a connection supercharged,
conductive. Wind blows, ready to siphon
electricity. Empedocles rated the forces
of nature into a quadrate of opposition.

Make Sugar When Drowning

Can't shut off a stained mind,
thoughts like tireless geese
wheel through the brain.

Make sugar, sweetness,
like birds laying eggs in
chili ristras.

Noah builds the ark,
each hammer blow
another's undoing,

historic disaster icon.

Mockingbird

A mockingbird near the veranda
convinces a starling they are brethren,
can share territory.

Backlit by sun, without trying,
they are falsely twinned, unlike effort
consumed to remake myself,
by then too complicated, too sad.
A river in a garden, a flat face
backs away from the door,
toes in a tub of sudsy winter.

No one connects this year.

Normal

You, the strained orange juice of my heart,
I, the blossom of your belly,
we, the dipped candle, say,
anyone can, anyhow, anywhen, anywhere.

You, normal corncob, growing
beside bamboo, stalking through
the forest, call to eagle overhead,
Skyhawk, come pluck me, silk
strand by kernel.   Dig roots from
dirt, fling my remains, an arrow,
at your next meal.

Ode to a Lost Poet

She sees gone things, connects
out of loneliness, loves anybody
each time. Tries to let go
of authority, her voice. Puts food
on the table, survival absolves
her, allows for violence, for sin.

Names fly from her mouth, toads,
wells sprout in her head. She sings
Billie Holiday, says, *The best poems*
are invented, the end in the middle,
a creativity creation generativity
generation manifestation refusal of invisibility.

For Mary she writes, *two apples, Havarti with dill,*
Swedish grains, green tea, an amethyst bracelet lost
in a porta-potty. She pulls poems from garbage,
nits off a Latin dog. Doesn't eat much
except chocolate.

She doesn't ask questions or need to know.
Mirabai and Marianne Moore dance around
the dead-poet pile. Poets don't smoke
tobacco anymore, too busy slowing down,
inner renunciation, self-contained moments,
self-acceptance

or officiousness, no quiet inside,
stammer, jagged, ribbed tongue
stimulated by interaction, burns
stupid hair straight, iron-on pants-
leg patches shine with poverty,
crazy lost physicality is spirit, is sex.

Iran, Iraq, all of Mesopotamia,
just family-exile countries. She
doesn't know where her soul comes
from, doesn't intend to find out
until the last possible moment.
A day owl hoots.

Ode to a Mexican Oracle

Objects hold power,
the bird in one hand,
the thing in the other.

A brown earthenware coffee set,
three mugs and serving pot, bought
in Mexico, Acapulco, 1980.
Our first real honeymoon, the first
of dozens of trips across
imaginary lines called borders.

Each cup, a stork or two, stark
white in green reeds along the bottom,
straight yellow beaks, black eyes
match the rims where we place our lips.

We love the serving set
more than we should. We knew
it knew all about what was to come.
Brown colored by white, yellow, black.

Ode to My Poets

Every shade of grey, absorbing me everyday,
like Dylan Thomas, so romantic, so rhythmic, so rhymed,
so dead. Wish I hadn't named my son for him,
wish I had named him instead for Marilyn Chin.
Or Gwendolyn Brooks, the EL clacking in the background,
iambic juice for her syncopated Chi-Town sound.

Or what of the turns we take,
anapest like *monkey cake*,
un-footed like William Carlos Williams
in his post-stroke streak, long-vowel-phase final days.
Or like love, a quick dance imploded by chance
or is it meant to last?

And what about you, Allen Ginsberg,
your picture on a book fallen to the bathroom floor?
And that damn backyard dove, that dolt, that daddy dove
taken down by a stub-for-a-tail, free-to-roam cat that
ran home, Doctor Seuss, to the two little girls
that I never had.

Pandora

What is this box of nail clippings, tissue,
    candle wax and cup rings?

What is this box of sobbing confusion
    and quiet cognition?

What is this box of bookshelves, clear crystal,
    animals curling and plants reaching?

What is this box of too much motion
    and no place to go?

What is this box of light from elsewhere
    and muffled birdsong?

What is this box of long silence, sudden argument,
    flashing color and worn carpet?

What is this box of providence, catastrophe
    and chaste sacrosanctity?

What is this box of plaster, lath,
    stucco and ochre paint?

Red Bird

Out of an empty sky, a red bird. Put pain
back where you found it. The last god,
ice shards, goulash, a cache of contraband.

Out of an empty ocean, a purple fish,
upsurge, refuge, scent of grandfathers,
of oxygen carried in blood, fills your head.

Every night between REM and light sleep,
Now-familiar multitudes wait for you,
beg, ready to unmake you.

Runes

I Division

Highway, dividing brain halves,
a void, a jump-over or dive-in
subconscious, unconscious, ultra conscious-

a black space full of empty, floating tokens.
Like Alice's rabbit hole, travel in wormholes,
swirl of vertigo, floating toast, mushrooms, keys,

shelves, bells, clocks, spinning tops.
Water cascades, falls in gorges, buries bones,
man's, mammoth's, midsummer moon.

II Vigilance

Children swim in turquoise.
Check after each turned page,
none have sunk. One shouts,

Help, I'm drowning. His father
snaps, *Never joke like that.*
The boy is a mind reader.

Wish for sleep. Who is watching
the baby girl, just out of diapers,
calling, *Mom, Mommy,*

I'm on the chair.
I'm not in the water.
No one answers.

III Vacation?

Walk from Santa Monica Pier to Venice Beach,
search for Rexroth's 100th -birthday celebration,
between lifeguard station twenty-one and twenty-nine.

Paper blinding in the light, go on write, deaf
to family play, bathe, squabble. Kites, footballs,
jugglers, skaters, bladers, seagulls, wind and surf—

riptide -- *No Barbeques, dogs, allowed.* Sand firm
near the shore, a choir on the bike path, pushing
muscles seldom used. Six miles in two hours.

Not bad or good, wind cools skin burnt
by sun. Know more tomorrow about this
pink-orange-pink Los Angeles day.

IV Resurrection

Write the light fantastic; do not stop, irreverent and irrelevant.
There is power in green chrysanthemums and sprouting lilac
shoes, adrift in a conundrum of one thousand words or much
less, alive in a shy, blue wedge of roots and wood. Toasted like
marshmallow runes. Feed birds, bring them for her pleasure
when sex reeks of repair work, empty paper twisted dry.

Sincerity

Alive, in the center, a shining mirror-
no game better than sincerity.
No gain feathered in eternity.

There are five of us.
We each reach for one truth
hidden in four sincere lies.

Of the twenty-five thoughts we share,
five are our truths, twenty fabrication,
misdirection, paintings in invisible ink.

Well, what did you think?
We can't all dare share a single
same or sane truth. In all sincerity

I offer the following five. One,
only one is a truth in my reality,
this now, or in my past or prior now.

I
If I had to do it over again,
I wouldn't change a thing.

II
I don't believe in secrets,
I have nothing to hide.

III
I am not afraid of my own death
but fear living through yours.

IV

We reap what we sow, make our own beds,
Karma always takes care of unfinished business.

V

None of this is exactly a lie, nor is any of it perfectly true

Remix

Trees fly beneath, between us.
Pigeons on the roof of a Conoco station,
not mating, castigating the smaller birds.

Remix—a new way to hear
Smell, touch an old thing,
taste the past with a forked tongue.

November dreams red fear,
unable to jump the abyss,
one wheel in mud.

Toothbrush scrubs a brain.
Yellow police ribbon, this year's
state flower, caught in clover.

Last night the moon lay
on its side, a peeled coconut half.
Who placed it the plain way today?

She Steps into the Forest

Little Red Riding Hood. Innocent.
Why does she wear a riding hood
when she walks to Grandmother's
house? Shouldn't she be herding
sheep and picking wild berries?

She is too virginal to see
into the darkness behind trees,
too narcissistic to feel eyes
following her or hear lips
smacking behind her on the path.

She does not notice when birds
call sharply before falling silent
and still on the limb.

Like a weasel, the wolf
inhabits her grandmother's body
and bed. Yet she pastes Grandmother's
visage under the expected nightcap,
sees the aging goddess, not the lupine –
nor does she scent his feral odor.
She leans in for a kiss.
Her wrists grabbed and stung by razor claws.
At last, her spilling blood alerts her.

Time to awaken, to become her own
Prince Charming, to rescue herself
from destruction, to climb out
of the sticky, stinking sludge.

Story Time

Unloved, the creative soul
journeys through synaptic juice.
Tells a story of three months
of light before the sun
blinks out one final time.
Darkness growls beyond control,
grabs the waste of chaos, sails
to storm's center. Waves feed
her on and off shore.

Moon falls into a dead earth fire.
Empowered by dinosaur bones and geode
stones, they answer questions about
how to make friends, babies, passage-
ways to great and small happinesses.
How to dance, shout, crawl and caw.

Pay attention to leaps, runs, crashes,
coughing, smashes, to explanations
and directions, to long tongued lizards,
rolling tickle games, autumn leaves.

Dirty parts of the world must also turn
to dust, howl themselves to sleep.

San Antonito

Sunset in San Antonito

A covey of distraction,
one foot afloat, blue
heron flock to the lake,
their backs a raft of sunset,
a boundary between air and
water.

Sky mirrored on surface,
cranes come in feetfirst,
slice a gate through night's
reflection. Stay until morning
or the next migratory cycle,
or the next buffalo pounded
drought.

Evening in San Antonito

In the restaurant, Patsy Cline,
a battle of cell phones, tie-
dyed shirts pinned on walls.
We spatter sibilants, hiss
like snakes, sing "happy birthday,"
laugh through drunken darkness,
lost on our way home.

Sunset Promises

Leave the bubbles and wand
on the table in the gazebo,
a promise to return next sunset.

Birds are silhouettes, end-of-day
racket, swift darting, sharp calls
mark their perfect branch.

Next sunset arrives, bereft
of bubble blowing. Legs stretch
out on the sofa after a day

on hardwood floors with new,
two-inch heels. Need cushions
and chamomile's comforts.

Open curtains, birds on the fence
tonight, like me. Do I get up?
Put something else on my feet?

Are the colors of clouds as brilliant
through dirty den windows? The air
inside is as still as I need to be tonight.

Bubbles and birds will be there tomorrow.

Tanta Rosa

In the kitchen on Hinman and Lake,
Tanta Rosa kept a jar of farmer
cheese and a pot of yogurt culturing.
What would she do now, with American
ovens and electronic ignitions, no slow
warmth of pilot lights to make these
staple foods? Cheese and cabbage with
a glass of brown vodka, yogurt and
potatoes with a glass of brown vodka,
beet borscht with sour cream and a glass
of brown vodka. She loved the bright-
yellow enameled pan my father cooked
his eggs in, would sit at the round
white kitchen table, feeling its smooth
surface, tapping the bottom, put it away
and pull out the five-quart, orange Dutch
oven, caress it, laugh with it, but never
use it. Glass jars culturing on top
of the oven, a ten-quart, Farberware
stainless-steel pot for everything else.
A small glass of tea with bergamot,
the same glass she used in the evening
for, yes, you guessed it, brown vodka.

Tanta means "Aunt"

Truth in Friendship

Clear to the bottom of deception lies a circular path where we practice a paper clip of truth, dance on boiling bubbles, stay afloat on unhinged facts.

At the command of crouching friendship, a soul sister coats herself in contraband, cotton candy, cumin-flavored observation in melting mirrors.

She counts on love to coin perception in a palatable, imperfect picture, can't be a cougar and expect love from a prince.

Slices herself open, cantaloupe tastes sweeter if salted. Decides what to do with the orange meat inside.

Raven: Don't look in Raven's eyes, deep, unlit cracks, a cave, all blackbirds can steal her soul, fear their beaks.

Borrow Raven's wings, flap inside her trapped wildness, fettered freedom.

Birded being, crevassed soul, taloned mortal, rib caged, impenetrable, invisible, armored existence,

share sorry truths. Tangerines plucked before ripeness never sweeten, soaked in sugar, bitterness penetrates.

Sit silently in musk, scream at brick walls, find the latest version of truth to throw at occluded mirrors.

Unflappable

She appears happy, an inchworm in her bra.
Water creatures bloom in her children's bones,
a consolation of lizards without tongues.

At her father's funeral, she plays a knife,
orange wedging into runaway shorts.
Her sister, the fork lodged in the chicken,
the newest constellation.

In recurrent, green-fruited dreams
oblong tornadoes follow Judas's goats
to open ocean. Wizard birds smash
eyes. Hurricanes, unhurried, form
unopposed, inflammable.

A Certain Brand of Polygamy

New Mexico borders the lust
state, the avarice state, the anger
state, where law enforcement turns
a blind ear to the other cheek,
where abandonment
is a normative action. Thirteen-year
old boys, also called competition, tossed
out on the streets. Like Stockholm Syndrome
victims, they want to work their way back
in, have a harem of underage death birds
to call their own, want to toss out their
own sons when the going gets pubescent.

Wedding Night in Arles, 1852

I pivot in front of the mirror—
not polished tin, real glass
swirl around in my good skirt,
until it lies askew over my
ready hips, as if I were a gypsy
girl instead of a milkmaid,
hat off, pulse pounding.

In the garden across from this fine
guest house, my olive-skinned
woodcutter paces like a mute
somnambulist, waits for me to pull
closed the shutters, his sign to join me.

Lovely, best wedding gift, one night
on a goose-down mattress, no bristly,
flat thatch, feathers piled high.

What Comes Next

Shaped into catastrophe,
I thirst to put knife to breast,
an exterior substance,
like sulphur and stink
to mark invisible wounds.

Or
I hunger to obliterate him,
carve a furious fissure
into his chest, remove his thirst
for young girls, ram a beehive
into the office of his heart.

Or
with luck, on a peacock's
rainbow feathers, vaporize
from this wicked corner,
reappear as the geometry
of rapture and release,
a mirror of sighs, my only vague
witness, a blossoming cherry tree.

Yellow Smoke

Triple star, double star, your yellow smoke
covers my town, what didn't burn last
year overflows with tinder and dry brush.

A Curve-Billed thrasher, mockingbird
and White-Winged dove thirst as they nest.
I scrape away Douglas-fir needles, trim
low and long branches to stave off ignition
points. The *cholla* blooms madly in fuchsia.

This unfastened evening, days before solstice,
a tanager flops off, wasted by heat. I burn,
can't get enough of throb, shake, breathe,
nest. Pollen falls from my faded T-shirt
near the yellow bleach spots on salmon-
colored cotton. With Round Mountain, Little
Bear, White Water, Baldy, and North Fire
combusting, I smoke without guilt, dream
of air rich with nicotine for all who wish
to inhale a breeze not laden with ash.

Transit of Venus no help at all, except
for John Philip Sousa's march of the same
name, while the muse opens a door buried
beneath stepped pyramids in Mexico
and the calendar of forever begins beckoning,
Come into the light, yellow and smoky.

Winter's Surreal Odyssey

For Art Goodtimes, our modern Ghalib

I

Reconcile the year, taxing friendships,
cook up tomorrow midday.
Earth revolves, we stand un-still,
a gust of feral flotsam, a pancake
of angst. Adornment, a line around the eyes,
leftover memory on the paternal side,
from a mini-separation anger tango.
Wild, wasted winter, wet test,
Frozen-fowl zone.

II

Thirteen of anything to an inch
spins small even in the elfin
arena. Another day of bird-
seed, steel sky snarls by the back
door. Upon return, envision
gold and garnet necklaces.

III

Dark-eyed boy cooks noodles and tofu
while you work. Life, not for practice,
paints 255 rectangles on a *shoji* screen,
sprouts swift as a comet.

IV

Fifteen degrees below zero,
clamp your hands, your soul
to untouchables all day. Drink
whiskey with tourists. Night
a slick pond of gray.

V

Alley of dreams ruptures,
dusted in black ash, in wet
turtles, box turtles, turtle toys,
dirt from under a childhood bed.
go to the loose place, to wild mind,
find this decade's Ghalib incarnation.
Wander a frosted desert, squawk
madly at ravens, softly at sparrows.
The poet's mask, no different than Janus,
than a vast and leaping heart. How did
Ghalib know we would read his words
two hundred years later?

VI

Like sitting in the dark, eyes closed,
reading Baba, eating tart plumb jam
with fingers. Today, a poet
not a house, you dance on the head
of a pin, spoon your way through verse,
close your throat over Ghalib,
another cancellation of air, of flightlessness.
Forget how to speak as stream of sound
discounting nights flow into eternity,
the next life and the next.

VII
How did we lose ourselves
in this loose and fragrant galaxy,
afraid the free mind might mean
madness or misery? We forget
to turn pages. Still, days flow
forward. We wonder, in the thick
of G-d's gifts, who might be Gabriel.
We forget how dirt becomes mud,
the devastating mother, we forget
trees cling here for climbing,
an adrenaline amp. We forget
Kali should wear blue.

VIII
When Sharp-Shin hawks rest on your fence,
conjure, crumble helpless beneath a fault line.
Miss the party at a crowded yellow house.
A ticket waits to be sold, breakfast congeals
on a table, a hometown meeting halfway across
a breadbasket. Slow hum fills air with lilac,
silence, minor anxiety. Walk
down a packed ochre road, western
slopes of the divide soar on the left.

The Basement

In the basement a four year old girl feeds a guinea pig.
In the basement a five year old girl walks through sewage.
In the basement a six year old girl watches an electrocution.

In the basement, a mockingbird opens its beak,
hopes its song will issue forth,
slams against a barred window.
Mockingbird can get free.

Your inner Bureau of Indian Affairs can get free.
Your inner burning hole can get free.
Your inner monkey-mind can get free.
Your too good child can get free.
Your celluloid wisdom can get free.
Your palette of denial can get free.
Your rotating mannequin can get free.

This year, opening beaks.
This year, broken eggs.
This year so few chips off the old block.
This year so much rhythm.
This year so little rhyme.
This year is like the sixties,
Tell it like it is, sock it to 'em.

Protest the war, globalization, The G-8, climate change,
deforestation, world hunger, anti-protest protesters.
A little girl comes up from the basement,
without guinea pig, her feet dry.

A Coincidence of Migration

Junco or sparrow, eagle or owl, thrasher or hummingbird?
It may turn out I am no bird at all.

In autumn, a nightjar gurgles high in her throat.

The time comes when pickled evil outlives her children
and her accomplices; anger and hate.
So much madness roots in denial of death, a seat
of crazy, of not getting past hurt. Left
with nothing, she transforms into a dove's egg,
fails to land in the nest, breaks on the sidewalk.

Words flutter, a yellow finch song, crowds
and cracking baseball bats, cricket chatter.

Mockingbirds have the largest avian vocabulary,
the poorest in-species communication, limited
to mating and alarm calls.

Ferocious kestrels protect first fledglings,
soar with them to tree limb's end.

How could the precious brown
speckled blue wren's eggs and nest
be torn form the tree, shredded?
Embryonic fluid and one unborn
in a dog's mouth and paw, two
inches of warm pink, a bitty
bright yellow beak.

ABOUT THE AUTHOR

Debbi Brody conducts poetry workshops and readings at festivals and other venues throughout the Southwest to writers age five through eighty-five. Her work has appeared in the Santa Fe Literary Review, Broomweed Journal, Poetica, Sin Fronteras and other regional and national magazines, journals and books of note including numerous anthologies. Her first full length collection, "Portraits in Poetry," (Village Books Press, Oklahoma 2006), as well as her chap-book,"FreeForm" are out of print. Her latest chapbook, "Awe in the Muddle," is available for order through artqueen58@aol.com. She is active in the poetry community, editing, writing and reviewing, coordinating readings and judging art shows and recitations. She is also employed by a small scientific research and development company. Debbi has lived in Santa Fe, NM with her husband since 1992.

CPSIA information can be obtained
at www.ICGtesting.com
Printed in the USA
FFOW03n1821110615
14079FF

9 781936 923137